THE BATTLE OF THE LITTLE BIGHORN

THE BATTLE OF THE LITTLE BIGHORN

BY MARTIN GITLIN

Content Consultant
Jeanne Eder, Ph.D.
University of Alaska–Anchorage

ABDO
Publishing Company

CREDITS

Published by ABDO Publishing Company, 8000 West 78th Street, Edina, Minnesota 55439. Copyright © 2008 by Abdo Consulting Group, Inc. International copyrights reserved in all countries. No part of this book may be reproduced in any form without written permission from the publisher. The Essential Library™ is a trademark and logo of ABDO Publishing Company.

Printed in the United States.

Editor: Andrew De Young
Copy Editor: Paula Lewis
Interior Design and Production: Emily Love
Cover Design: Emily Love

Library of Congress Cataloging-in-Publication Data

Gitlin, Martin.
  The Battle of the Little Bighorn / Martin Gitlin.
      p. cm. — (Essential events)
  Includes bibliographical references.
  ISBN 978-1-60453-045-2
  1. Little Bighorn, Battle of the, Mont., 1876—Juvenile literature.
  2. Dakota Indians—Wars—Juvenile literature. I. Title.

  E83.876.G54 2008
  973.8'2—dc22

                              2007031208

TABLE OF CONTENTS

Indian ceremonies such as the Sun Dance are still held today.

ON THE TRAIL TO A SHOWDOWN

It was June 1876. A full moon lit the sky. Sitting Bull, the revered Lakota Sioux medicine man, prepared to speak to the Great Spirit. The Sioux believed that all things had a living spirit, and that spirit was called *Wakan Tanka*. Sitting

Bull and his fellow Plains tribesmen prayed to the Great Spirit, embodied in the mystic powers of the earth, sun, moon, and stars. Their prayer, offered during the Sun Dance, asked the Great Spirit for a bountiful year. As part of the 12-day ceremony, warriors offered flesh from their bodies as a sacrifice. Sitting Bull remained still as brother Jumping Bull sliced 50 pieces of flesh off each of Sitting Bull's arms. That ritual fulfilled a promise Sitting Bull had made months earlier, after he had ridden his horse deep into the Black Hills of Dakota Country—the *Paha Sapa*.

In the Black Hills, Sitting Bull had loosened the braids of his long black hair. He placed tobacco in his clay pipe, around which he wound wild sage, a sacred herb of his people. As he smoked his pipe and was filled with the scent of tobacco and wild sage, he prayed to *Wakan Tanka* in song:

> *Grandfather behold me!*
>
> *Grandfather behold me!*
>
> *I hold my pipe and offer it to you.*
>
> *That my people may live.*[1]

Population Explosion

While the Indian population was rapidly shrinking in the mid-1800s, the initial wave of immigration from Europe had drastically expanded the white population. In the 100 years after the signing of the Declaration of Independence in 1776, the overall U.S. population expanded from 3 million to 44 million.

It was an understandable request. The American Indian population had decreased from an estimated 1 million to 300,000 since the signing of the Declaration of Independence gave birth to the United States of America 100 years earlier.

The buffalo, which had once freely roamed the plains, had always been the lifeblood of the Indians. The white man's slaughtering of the buffalo had caused great hardship. Along with diseases brought by white settlers and war with the U.S. Army, the slaughtering of buffalo caused a dramatic decrease in tribal populations.

Yes, Sitting Bull had much to pray for on his journey through the Black Hills. It was on that day that he promised to sacrifice 100 pieces of flesh to the Great Spirit. He hoped to receive a great vision in return.

As the Sioux warrior performed the Sun Dance weeks later, he was rewarded with the vision of hundreds of Bluecoat soldiers and traitor Indian scouts falling from the sky into the camp. He believed the Great Spirit was giving his people a historic victory because the white people had refused to accept that the sacred Black Hills were meant to belong to the American Indians. He spoke to the other Lakota Sioux, who agreed. Sitting Bull and his people were destined to achieve a great triumph.

THE OTHER SIDE

Miles away, however, those "Bluecoats" were just as certain that the Indians they pursued were destined for a devastating defeat.

Angered by the Indians' refusal to sell the Black Hills, the U.S. government commanded the army to convince the Indians to leave Dakota Country and return to their reservations. If the Indians refused, they were to be considered hostile, and all measures to drive them back to the reservations would be taken.

Army Lieutenant General Philip Sheridan ordered groups of soldiers, commanded by General George Crook, General Alfred Terry, and Colonel John Gibbon, to converge

Hardtack

Hardtack was among the most convenient foods the U.S. Cavalry ate during their search for hostiles. The hard cracker or biscuit remained edible for extended periods of time, which allowed soldiers to take it along for long rides. Hardtack became popular among Confederate soldiers during the Civil War.

on areas occupied by hostile tribes. The plan was to surround the Indians and defeat them in battle.

The first skirmish occurred in March 1876 when six companies of Crook's soldiers attacked the peaceful Cheyenne camp of Chief Two Moons. The camp was overwhelmed. They attempted to fight but were forced to flee as the troops killed many tribe members and burned the entire village.

The Cheyenne fled downstream along the Powder River to a Lakota Sioux camp led by Crazy Horse. The

Fighting for the "Other Side"

Not all American Indians banded together for a common cause against white settlers and the U.S. Army.

Traditional enemies of the Lakota Sioux and Cheyenne such as the Crow, Shoshone, and Arikara served as scouts to help the soldiers track down hostiles and fought on the side of the cavalry. An estimated 200 Crow and Shoshone saved General Crook from even greater defeat in the Battle at Rosebud Creek in 1876.

One of the reasons the Crow and Arikara fought with the soldiers was that their tribes had been defeated years earlier on the Northern Plains.

The Arikara were more inclined to assimilate into white society. Chief White Shield expressed their feelings:

It has been prophesized that a people of different skin color would be coming and would change our way of living. They are here now, so we will have to learn to live with them and learn their language, go to school, so we can live in their world. We know that our way of life will be gone.[2]

Of course, other American Indians argued that whites had no right to push their way of life on them. Those who felt that way continued to fight for their land and for their way of life.

bands traveled together for strength in numbers. They hunted buffalo along the 60-mile (97-km) route north to Sitting Bull's village. Once they arrived, they discovered that other American Indians had joined the camp.

From One War to Another

Many of the soldiers who were commissioned to track down and fight the Sioux and other tribes in the 1860s and 1870s had fought in the Civil War. Some were career soldiers who simply went from one war to another in order to make money.

One month later, Terry's troops began their search for hostiles. Among his leaders was George Armstrong Custer, a Civil War hero driven by personal glory. Custer had slaughtered more than 100 Cheyenne in a massacre at the Battle of Washita eight years earlier. He was eager to further establish his reputation as an Indian fighter.

In search of hostiles, Terry sent six regiments led by Custer and Major Marcus Reno to the Rosebud River. Indian scouts spotted U.S. Army troops and reported back to their camps. Sitting Bull and other leaders became certain an attack was imminent.

The Battle of Rosebud Creek

The Sioux avenged the attack at Powder River in mid-June with an attack of their own at Rosebud Creek. Sioux and Cheyenne scouts had found Crook

Religious Differences

One segment of the American population felt morally obligated to "civilize" the American Indians. They felt driven to educate the Indians in Christian beliefs, but the vast majority in the various tribes felt no desire to change. Instead, they had a religious worldview that was tied to the land.

and his group en route to Rosebud Valley. At mid-morning, the soldiers were shocked to see a band of Sioux riding down upon them. The six-hour battle left Crook's men soundly defeated.

Crook would not be able to continue his mission. Instead, he tended to the wounded. Unfortunately, his fellow army leaders had no way of knowing that Crook's group had been defeated. Meanwhile, more Indian warriors continued to join Sitting Bull. The odds were being stacked in the Indians' favor.

The Battle of the Little Bighorn was on the horizon. But the conflicts between whites and American Indians had begun the moment European explorers set foot on American soil.

Sioux religious leader Sitting Bull

Italian explorer Christopher Columbus "discovered" America while looking for a route to the East Indies.

AMERICAN INDIANS MEET NEW AMERICANS

For decades, American children have been taught that Christopher Columbus discovered America in 1492. But how could he truly discover a land that was already populated? In 1492, an estimated 5 million American Indians already occupied what is now known as the United States.

THE FIRST AMERICANS

Some scientists say that American Indians came from Russia, crossing a land bridge in Alaska before spreading out into North and South America. Other people say that the American Indians were always on these continents. Both agree that Indians were in America thousands of years before Columbus set sail.

Columbus was an Italian explorer commissioned by Spain to find a faster route to the East Indies. When he came upon the North American continent, he and his crew believed they had reached their destination, which is why they named the natives Indians.

The explorers were amazed by the appearance and lifestyle of the natives, which was different than anything they had ever seen. Most of

The First Thanksgiving

The American Indians contributed to a celebration by the Pilgrims in fall 1621, the year after they landed at Plymouth Rock. The Indians had taught the white settlers how to plant corn in hills and use fish as a fertilizer. The corn crop proved successful. This prompted the 50 colonists to invite the Indians to the celebration. Pokanoket tribe leader Massasoit and 90 men represented the Wampanoag tribe. This celebration of thanks was not given the name Thanksgiving Day until years later.

the natives lived as farmers and occasional hunters in the southeast, northeast, and eastern part of the Midwest. They often used sign language to communicate.

CULTURES COLLIDE

Until European settlers brought horses, the American Indians walked from place to place, using dogs to pull their gear. Hunting tribes such as the Sioux, Comanche, and Cheyenne eventually obtained horses through trading and stealing, which allowed them to move to the area between the Mississippi River and Rocky Mountains otherwise known as the Plains. The Indian tribes often fought each other for horses and land.

The use of horses dramatically altered the lifestyle of the American Indians. No longer limited to one area, they were able to roam huge areas of land. They no longer had to hunt on foot. Tribesmen easily killed buffalo, millions of which wandered the Plains.

Sign Language

Just like people from different countries, American Indians of different nations spoke different languages. To communicate with each other, they often used sign language. The initial sign upon contact with another tribe was to rub the left hand twice. A specific sign then identified what tribe the signer was from.

Hunting buffalo provided a way of life for Plains Indians.

Buffalo were the life source of the Indians. They were not only used for food; their hides were used to create clothing and teepees. The buffalo's hair was shorn to make pillows. The buffalo provided everything they needed to survive.

The coming of European settlers also introduced the Indians to guns, and these soon became a valuable commodity. Though hunters and warriors had become experts at the rapid firing of arrows, guns were far more effective in the hunting of buffalo and in warring against rival tribes.

By the 1800s, many Indians had migrated to the Plains. They enjoyed freedom with few restrictions aside from those placed upon them by other tribes. They believed the land they had adopted was rightfully theirs.

But so did the white settlers. Many settlers hoped to live in peace with the Indians as they began their journeys west. They believed there was plenty of land for everyone. Others thought that these Indians with strange ways and customs had no rights to prevent their migration to any territory. They referred to the Indians as "savages" or "red devils." Some settlers hoped to transform, educate, and convert the Indians into Christians and "modernize" their way of life.

Buffalo

American Indians did not simply hunt buffalo for food, clothing, and items such as bed covers, saddles, and tools. They also extracted the blood of the buffalo to use as body paint. The buffalo was so critical to their lives that the Indians often gave thanks to the Great Spirit for providing an animal with such great abundance.

The Europeans came to America with a different concept of the land. They believed that individuals could own pieces of land. The American Indians, however, had a communal style of living and believed that the land was for everyone. Some tribes believed that those who walked barefoot on the soil soaked up the earth's healing powers. They felt that "Mother Earth" was a gift from the Great Spirit.

Though some Indians welcomed the assimilation into the white

Sioux Sidelights

No American-Indian nation has a more storied history or was more entrenched in a fight for survival than the Sioux. But not all Sioux tribes became involved in the battles of the mid-to-late 1800s. Those noted warriors were members of the Teton division.

The Sioux were divided into three divisions, each of which had various tribes. Teton (Western) Sioux were separated into seven tribes: the Oglala, Brule, Hunkpapa, Sihasapa, Miniconjou, Oohenonpa, and Itazipco.

The Nakota (Middle) Sioux were divided into the Yankton, Yankonia, Hunkpatina, and Assiniboine tribes.

The Santee (Eastern) Sioux consisted of the Mdewakanton, Wahpeton, Wahpekute, and Sisseton tribes.

The Sioux were not given permanent personal names until they had earned them. Before earning his name, one young Oglala tribesman was known as Light-Skinned Boy for his distinct complexion. His father's name was Crazy Horse. The elder Crazy Horse did not transfer his name until his son earned it in battle. After transferring his name to his son, the elder Crazy Horse became known as Worm.

Another child was nicknamed Slow and formally known as Jumping Badger. When he earned his father's respect as a warrior, he earned the name Sitting Bull.

settler's world, most did not. They resented the idea that they should give up their culture. The concept of coexistence began to crumble in the mid-1800s. The intrusion of settlers into what Indians considered their territory caused friction. So did the dramatically decreasing number of buffalo, which were often killed by settlers merely for the sport or novelty.

Throughout the eighteenth century and well into the nineteenth century, white settlers saw little reason to migrate westward. Many believed the West was an empty land dominated by desert. Word eventually spread from those who did make the difficult journey that the territory west of the Mississippi River boasted fertile land for farming.

As the number of settlers, adventurers, and miners moving westward increased, so did clashes with the Indians. Battles occurred throughout the Plains in an area reaching from present-day Minnesota and Montana to as far south as Oklahoma and as far west as Colorado. Meanwhile, tribes in other areas of America were having their own battles with white settlers and the U.S. government.

Soon the differences in philosophy and culture became apparent in the fighting styles. Soldiers followed strict guidelines and chains of command.

They were professionals fighting not only for pay, but also for the country and for their regiments. They took a scientific approach to battle, looking for advantages in numbers and ammunition.

The Indian warriors were well-versed in the tactics of fighting on the plains. Many would follow the lead of Crazy Horse, who was their military commander. His war tactics became so famous that cadets still study them at the U.S. Military Academy at West Point.

Neither side was accustomed to the type of warfare that became prevalent. Neither the army nor the various tribes often knew where they could locate the enemy. Scouts were used by both sides. It was wide-open warfare in which surprise attacks against completely unprepared enemies were common.

Many tribes became involved in conflicts against the U.S. soldiers.

The Sioux

The Sioux were a mobile group who were unafraid to raid other tribes for what they needed. They were particularly aggressive with the Shoshone tribe. One Sioux raid on the Shoshone in 1841 resulted in the capture of many horses.

The entire American-Indian population was adversely affected by the influx of white people and their westward migration. But the Sioux and Cheyenne fought the most significant battles in what can best be described as a war against the United States.

When greed took over with the 1849 Gold Rush, the white stampede to the West began in earnest. And so did the war. ⌣

Many of the white settlers moving into Indian land made the journey in covered wagons, such as these replicas.

*Sutter's Mill, where the discovery of gold sparked
the California Gold Rush*

BROKEN TREATIES,
HEIGHTENED TENSION

At first, the word trickled back East.
Then the story hit like a flood. Gold
had been discovered in California. The rush to the
West was on.

It was 1848. Both to new immigrants and to families who had roots in one area for generations, the temptation was overwhelming. The hopeful prospectors began the long journey to California. Though they were nicknamed "49ers" because many began mining for gold in 1849, the westward migration in the search for gold continued far longer.

The gold seekers not only trespassed on territory American Indians considered their own, but they also brought diseases that took a toll on tribal populations. They also killed thousands of buffalo along the way, leaving the Indians starving, angry, and thirsty for revenge.

Many white settlers had traveled west of the Mississippi River several years before the California Gold Rush, seeking new homes. They were unaware that they were on Indian soil.

The Cheyenne were most affected because their villages

Andrew Jackson

Though some American leaders believed in peaceful coexistence with the American Indians, President Andrew Jackson was not among them. A decade before the white migration west, Jackson had predicted and favored the destruction of the American Indians. "Those tribes [cannot] exist surrounded by our settlements and in continual contact with our citizens," Jackson said in 1832. "They have neither the intelligence, the industry, the moral habits, nor the desire of improvement. ... They must necessarily yield to the first of circumstance and, ere long, disappear."[1]

peppered the areas most frequently traversed by settlers and gold seekers. All the Plains tribes were affected, and they could not get the U.S. military to help with the problem. Soon, they took matters into their own hands and attacked wagon trains.

A Peaceful Compromise?

The U.S. government needed a solution to soothe the relationship between the settlers and the Indians. Thomas Fitzpatrick was selected to create a peaceful compromise. As a government

Indian Slavery

At the same time that blacks were being enslaved by their white masters in the South, American Indians were being sold into slavery in the West.

After white gold seekers began staking their claims in California in 1850, more than 10,000 Indians were used as slaves in the mining industry. The white miners had no respect for the tribesmen, whom they called "diggers" for their practice of gathering roots.

Not only were tribesmen sold into slavery, but the women were used as slaves around the home, and children often were abducted. It was not until 1869—four years after black slavery was outlawed in the United States—that Indian slavery was banned in California.

In May 1850, the same year California became a state, five Pomo tribesmen who had killed their white slave owners were sought by U.S. troops. When the army detachment could not find their prey, they ordered the killing of a group of Pomos who were innocently fishing in Clear Lake.

The Pomos attempted to surrender, but the soldiers were in no mood to take prisoners. Instead, the soldiers went to the Indian camp and murdered 130 Pomos, mostly women and children. Similar incidents were not uncommon in California.

agent based in Wyoming Territory, Fitzpatrick had been protective of the American Indians. He was sincere in his desire to reach a mutual agreement. Leaders in Washington, D.C., believed Fitzpatrick was an ideal mediator.

Fitzpatrick arranged for 10,000 American Indians to gather at Horse Creek, approximately 35 miles (56 km) from Fort Laramie, near where he was stationed. This was the largest number of tribesmen ever assembled and included Sioux, Cheyenne, Arikara, Arapaho, Shoshone, and Crow chiefs.

The U.S. government had drawn up a treaty it hoped would appease the various tribes. It agreed to give the tribes who signed the agreement $50,000 for the next 50 years, as well as guns, food, and other goods, in return for free access to certain territory on which the U.S. government and citizens could travel and build roads.

The Indians who attended the ceremony believed an era of harmony between their peoples and white

The Cherokees

Among the tribes most willing to assimilate into white culture were the Cherokees, who resided mostly in the South, particularly in the state of Georgia. Missionaries educated and Christianized the Cherokees in the early 1800s. By 1828, the Cherokees had their own newspaper, the *Cherokee Phoenix*. It was printed both in English and Sequoyah, a language named after a tribesman who devised a new Cherokee alphabet in 1821.

America was about to begin. Arapaho tribesman Cut Nose said,

> I will go home satisfied. I will sleep sound and not have to watch my horses in the night, or be afraid for my squaws and children. We have to live on these streams and in the hills, and I would be glad if the whites would pick out a place for themselves and not come into our grounds. [2]

The Senate later cut the agreement to ten years without informing the tribes who had signed it.

The Treaty of 1851 also restricted hunting to certain areas in which no white man nor rival tribe could trespass. Tribes could hunt or fish outside those boundaries if they wanted to, as long as they stayed away from white travel routes. The American Indians could live outside their reservations, but in essence it was a way for the U.S. government to keep the Indians in designated areas. The treaty also outlawed raiding, which particularly hindered the Sioux and Cheyenne. Both tribes had used the practice against their rivals not only as a means to procure horses but also to bring honor to individuals.

Eating Buffalo

How did the decreasing number of buffalo on the plains relate to starvation among American Indians? It has been estimated that more than 100 people could be fed from the meat of one buffalo.

*Comanche and Arapaho tribespeople discuss what to do about
white encroachment on their land.*

The Treaty of 1851 forced tribes whose chiefs
had signed it to become greatly dependent on the
American government. It angered many who believed

Westward expansion brought white settlers into conflict with
Plains Indians. Here, a group of Indians raids a wagon train.

the Indians were perfectly capable of being self-
sufficient if white people and the U.S. government
did not destroy the lifestyles of the Indian cultures.

In 1853, a similar treaty was signed by the
Comanche and Kiowa tribes, who agreed to allow
whites to pass on the Santa Fe Trail in return for
$18,000 in supplies.

THE BROKEN TREATIES

Both treaties were doomed to fail. Not only did
the tribes rightfully believe the treaty remained in

place for 50 years, but their chiefs did not speak for all of their tribes. Other Indians either did not fully understand or simply ignored the requirements of the treaty, which included severe limits to buffalo hunting grounds. Raids between tribes continued.

The supplies provided to the tribes by the U.S. government were wholly inadequate. Starvation continued to plague the American Indians. Their population had decreased to 400,000 from the estimated 5 million when European explorers first set foot on North American soil.

The scarcity of food forced tribes to go outside their designated areas, which caused greater friction between tribal members and European settlers. The Army responded by sending more troops out West.

The first battle between the Plains Indians and the Unites States was provoked when the Sioux warrior

Other Tribes

While the Sioux and Cheyenne tribes remained strong into the second half of the nineteenth century, northern tribes such as the Shawnee, Miami, Ottawa, Huron, and Delaware had been subdued and often pushed westward by white settlers. When they arrived west of the Mississippi, these once strong tribes looked shabby compared to the Sioux and Cheyenne, both of which had yet to be greatly affected by white expansion.

High Forehead killed a cow that a white settler on the Oregon Trail had either left or abandoned. The owner of the cow returned and demanded $25 as reparation for the loss of the cow. Sioux leader Bear That Scatters offered two cows, but the army insisted on High Forehead's arrest.

On August 17, 1854, Army Lieutenant John L. Grattan led 31 of his men into the Sioux camp. Bear That Scatters refused to allow High Forehead to be arrested. This prompted Grattan to order his men to fire into the village. Bear That Scatters was hit and within seconds Lakota warriors rushed into battle and killed all 32 men. Bear That Scatters died later from his wounds. This marked the first time troops had been killed in what can be described as a U.S.-Indian battle.

However, it would not be the last time. In the next several decades, thousands would die in battle on both sides. ⌐

As the white people moved westward, they decimated the buffalo and
destroyed the way of life for the Plains Indians.

Famous warrior Crazy Horse will be honored by a huge sculpture in the Black Hills.

LET THEM EAT GRASS

year had passed since provoked Sioux tribesmen along the Oregon Trail wiped out an army group led by Army Lieutenant John Grattan. But the army was not about to forget.

The Fighting Continues

A regiment under the command of Brigadier-General William S. Harney was sent to a Sioux camp on Blue Water Creek in Nebraska. The soldiers killed 86 Indians and destroyed the village. A Sioux boy named Curly watched the massacre from a nearby hillside. He rode into the Sand Hills to find a vision. He saw himself riding on a flying horse as bullets and arrows flew by. The boy told the vision to his father, who explained it meant that he would become a great warrior who would avenge the atrocities committed by the white man. That boy would soon become known as Crazy Horse.

Crazy Horse and Sitting Bull attended a meeting of Lakota Sioux in 1857. Nearly 10,000 Lakota gathered in the Black Hills to discuss the continued white migration to the West. The Sioux reinforced their belief that the Black Hills area was rightfully theirs and that they would continue to fight against white intruders.

Crazy Horse

A sculpture of Sioux Chief Crazy Horse carved out of a mountain in the Black Hills began taking shape in 1948 and is still being created. Sculptor Korczak Ziolkowski worked on it until he passed away in 1982, but his family has since taken over the project. The completed sculpture of Crazy Horse on his horse will be the largest sculpture in the world at 567 by 641 feet (173 m by 195 m). It stands near the Mount Rushmore carvings of Presidents George Washington, Thomas Jefferson, Abraham Lincoln, and Theodore Roosevelt.

Soon the Cheyenne would be put to the test. When gold was discovered in Colorado in 1859, miners set up camps in Cheyenne territory. Thousands of eager whites streamed in and made homes on tribal land. This migration is responsible for the early prosperity of the city of Denver.

Three years later, construction began on the first railroad that would connect the East and West coasts of the United States, which would attract more whites to the central Plains.

THE SANTEE MASSACRE

Frustration among the Santee Sioux in Minnesota had been growing for years as 150,000 whites settled on their lands in the 1850s. In addition, money and food supplies promised by the U.S. government failed to arrive, which fueled hunger and anger in the Santee Sioux tribe.

Santee tribesman Big Eagle said,

> The whites were always trying to make the Indians give up their life and live like white men—go to farming, work hard and do as they did—and the Indians did not know how to do that, and did not want to anyway. If the Indians had tried to make the whites live like them, the whites would have resisted,

and it was the same way with many Indians. ... Many of the white men often abused the Indians and treated them unkindly. Perhaps they had excuse, but the Indians did not think so. Many of the whites always seemed to say by their manner when they saw an Indian, "I am better than you," and the Indians did not like this. ... The Dakota [Sioux] did not believe there were better men in the world than they.²

One person who treated the Santee badly was storekeeper Andrew Myrick. When the Santee could no longer pay for food at his shop because the government had not paid them and they began starving, he refused to give them food.

Santee Chief Little Crow said to government agent Thomas Galbraith,

We have waited a long time. The money is ours, but we cannot get it. We have no food, but here are these stores, filled with food. We ask that you, the agent, make some arrangement by which we can get food from the stores, or else we may take our own way to keep ourselves from starving. When men are hungry they help themselves.

The Massacre's Aftermath

More than 2,000 Santee were arrested following the massacre in Minnesota. They were brought to a trial in which 307 of them were sentenced to death. President Lincoln commuted the sentences of those simply found guilty of participating in battle, but 38 were hanged. This is the largest mass hanging in the history of the United States.

Galbraith turned to Myrick, who snapped, "If they are hungry, let them eat grass!"[3]

Anger soon reached a boiling point in 1862. After several Santee killed five settlers, others in the tribe went on a rampage. They murdered an estimated 500 whites over the next five days. One of them was Myrick.

CONFLICT ON THE PLAINS

In the meantime, the flimsy Treaty of 1851 continued to show its weaknesses. White travelers flocked through the Black Hills, which were sacred to tribes such as the Lakota Sioux. Though the agreement allowed for roads and forts to be built in the area, the Indians believed it had banned all whites from their sacred grounds.

The discovery of gold in Montana also prompted white migration in the central Plains. Battles between the whites and Sioux, led by Oglala warrior Red Cloud, became more frequent. Gold miners and settlers on the Bozeman Trail, which ran from the northern Plains through Wyoming and into Montana, traveled at great risk.

Another issue with the Treaty of 1851 was that American Indians often did not receive the money and supplies they were promised. The situation worsened in the early 1860s when the Civil War took the attention of the government away from its obligations. Tribes who were ignored and often hungry became increasingly

White Sympathizers

The conflicts between whites and American Indians in the Plains were actually welcomed by some tribes. The Crow and Arikara had suffered from Sioux aggression for generations, including raids that ended in the stealing of horses and other valuable items. This helped the U.S. government convince Crow and Arikara tribesmen to help the army as scouts and warriors against the Sioux. The Crow and Arikara, however, did not realize that they were also destined to be victims of white expansion.

Settlers who traveled the Bozeman Trail faced a dangerous trip through rough, mountainous territory.

angered at white trespassers with full stomachs and all the provisions they needed.

One leader who tried to maintain peaceful relations was Cheyenne Chief Black Kettle. But unlike the American army, tribesmen were not obligated to obey their commanding officer. Cheyenne leaders found it difficult to control the younger warriors, who attacked wagon trains and white settlements.

EVANS, CHIVINGTON, AND THE HUNDRED DAZERS

Colorado Governor John Evans finally declared war on the American Indians in 1864. He ordered the Cheyenne and Arapaho to relocate to a reservation where they would be provided with everything they needed. Evans wanted to separate the friendly Indians from the hostile Indians, who would then be hunted down.

Evans ordered Colonel John Chivington to lead the fight. Chivington, who hated American Indians, organized an unruly mob that was called the Third Colorado Regiment. It was better known as the Hundred Dazers for its short enlistment time.

When asked to meet with Black Kettle, who hoped to negotiate a peaceful settlement, Evans said with disdain, "But what shall I do with the Third Colorado Regiment if I make

The Crowded Cities

Another reason for the vast white westward migration of the mid-1850s was simply that the major eastern cities were becoming crowded. The population of the United States in 1840 was approximately 20 million, but immigrants were flooding in from Europe and Asia. Many people who lived in cities such as New York, Philadelphia, and Boston wanted to escape the noise and bustle of the city by moving west.

peace? They have been raised to kill Indians, and they must kill Indians."[4]

It was too late. Black Kettle and his fellow tribesmen had already traveled 400 miles (644 km) to speak with Evans. Black Kettle pleaded with the governor to work toward peace, but Evans charged him wrongly with conspiring with the Sioux, who had joined hostile Cheyenne in attacking white travelers.

The Cheyenne and Arapaho eventually settled down around Sand Creek in Indiana and were receiving food and provisions from government officials led by Major Edward W. Wynkoop. The American Indians trusted Wynkoop, but he was soon relieved of his duties and replaced by Chivington, who had recently told his soldiers to kill every Indian they came across. They would soon do just that.

Colorado Governor John Evans declared war on the American Indians,
sparking events that would lead to a massacre.

Chivington's soldiers charge into Black Kettle's village.

Massacre
at Sand Creek

The Cheyenne at Sand Creek were now
peaceful, but Chivington was not one
to make peace when war was expected of him. The
colonel was not happy when Black Kettle and other
Cheyenne settled peacefully at Sand Creek. The 100

days for the Hundred Dazers were running out. He had been commissioned to kill Indians, and he was determined to do exactly that.

A Shocking Massacre

Chivington's soldiers expressed shock when he told them of his plans to attack the Cheyenne at Sand Creek. In the early morning on November 29, 1864, he and approximately 700 soldiers traveled 40 miles (64 km) from the fort to Sand Creek. They awoke the natives at dawn to the frightful sound of gunfire.

Black Kettle immediately raised a white flag of surrender, but Chivington was not interested in peace. He and his men attacked the unarmed American Indians—including women and children.

An interpreter at the village said,

> They were scalped, their brains knocked out; the men used their knives ... [and] knocked them in the head with their guns, beat their brains out, mutilated their bodies in every sense of the word.[1]

By the time the slaughter was over, more than 200 Cheyenne were dead. Black Kettle survived the massacre, only to be killed four years later in a similar incident by a regiment led by George Custer.

Custer would later be a principle character at the Battle of the Little Bighorn.

Chivington reveled in his glory. He and his troops were heroes in Denver, where he marched triumphantly through the streets with his men. Chivington later entertained the audience with stories about the incident and displayed 100 Indian scalps on a Denver stage.

When the truth of the massacre was revealed, however, the public became disgusted with Chivington and

Warning from a General

William Tecumseh Sherman was best known for his exploits as a general fighting for the North during the Civil War. He is famous for leading his troops to capture Atlanta and burning down the city, though he claimed a smaller fire was intended, but it got out of control.

After the South was defeated in the Civil War, Sherman turned his attention to taming the West. He expressed contempt for the American Indians whom he believed needed to be eliminated so white expansion could be completed.

Sherman's views were clearly stated in a letter he wrote in October 1868 to General Sheridan, whom he was commissioning to lead a fight against the Plains Indians:

I will say nothing and do nothing to restrain our troops from doing what they deem proper on the spot, and will allow no vague general charges of cruelty and inhumanity to tie their hands.

[But I will] use all the powers confided to me to the end that these Indians, the enemies of our race and of our civilization, shall not again be able to begin and carry out their barbarous warfare on any kind of pretext they may choose to allege.[2]

his troops. The U.S. Congress set up several investigations and tried to work up a new plan to keep peace with the American Indians. Nothing was going to work at that point, however, especially among the Cheyenne, Sioux, and Arapaho in the West. The massacre at Sand Creek had been perpetrated against peaceful people. The tribesmen were convinced more than ever that whites could not be trusted, particularly those representing the U.S. government.

The Massacre's Aftermath

Some Cheyenne sought revenge, stepping up their attacks on white settlers. Others joined the Sioux and fellow Cheyenne who were based along the Powder River. When the government called for a council at Fort Laramie in June 1866 to discuss peace along the Bozeman Trail, Sioux Chief Red Cloud and other chiefs agreed to attend.

The Homestead Act

The U.S. government did not keep the feelings of the American Indians in mind when it passed the Homestead Act on May 20, 1862. It granted 160 acres of free land to anyone who wished to settle in the West. Those who took the offer only had to pay $1.25 per acre after a six-month period. The legislation helped create a mass migration, particularly to Kansas, where about 30,000 claims were made by 1871.

Over a century after the massacre, American Indians want a memorial to remember those killed at Sand Creek.

Government negotiator E.B. Taylor offered the
tribes access to the hunting grounds, along with
money, guns, and other provisions. But Taylor
indicated nothing about the plans to build forts
along the Bozeman Trail to protect white travelers.
When that was revealed by Colonel Henry B.

Carrington, Red Cloud reacted angrily:

> *The Great Father sends us presents and wants us to sell him the road, but the white chief goes with soldiers to steal the road before the Indians say yes or no!*[3]

Red Cloud and others, angered at what they considered to be deceitful tactics, stormed off. But Taylor convinced other Sioux and Cheyenne to sign an agreement allowing white settlers to pass through Indian territory on the Bozeman Trail.

The agreement was worthless. Attacks against white travelers became more fierce, and three forts were built along the trail. Following construction of the forts, Red Cloud and his fellow warriors increased their attacks in numbers and ferocity.

Among the forts built by Carrington was Fort Kearny. Troops trekked out daily to cut timber and bring it back to the fort. The

A Deadly Encounter

During one hunting trip in the late summer of 1867, a group of Sioux and Cheyenne came across a set of railroad tracks. Tribesman Sleeping Rabbit suggested they bend the track and spread it out, then wait for the train. The train derailed and all but two passengers were killed. The Indians stole sacks of flour, sugar, and coffee. They set the boxcars on fire and rode away before soldiers could catch them.

troops were also attacked daily, so Carrington sent a force led by Captain William Fetterman in December 1866 to chase off the Sioux.

Carrington could not have picked a more belligerent man. Fetterman bragged he could destroy the Sioux with 80 men, which is the number he gathered up. He expressed a lack of respect for the fighting ability of the Plains Indians. Fetterman foolishly ordered his men over a hill, where approximately 2,000 Cheyenne and Oglala Sioux, including Crazy Horse, were waiting.

The entire regiment was destroyed. One civilian who had decided to join the fight was found with 105 arrows in him. At the risk of being captured alive, Fetterman committed suicide.

Sioux leader White Bull recalled,

Sioux Chief Gall

Among the Sioux's toughest and strongest warriors was Chief Gall. In the mid-1860s, soldiers who had come to arrest him for horse stealing stabbed him many times through his body and once through the neck with their bayonets. They kicked him repeatedly while he lay on the ground. Thinking he was dead, they threw him in a nearby ravine. Not only did Gall recover, but he also survived to play a major role at the Battle of the Little Bighorn a decade later.

At Fort Laramie, pivotal peace talks were held between Indians and the U.S. government.

The Indians kept riding around, hanging on the sides of their horses, loosing arrows at the infantry, and there were so many of them that the fight with the infantry did not last long. But it lasted long enough to kill and wound a number of Indians and their horses.[4]

The Sioux and Cheyenne celebrated a victory. But eight months later they would be lamenting defeat. Soldiers armed with a new rapid-firing rifle that shot longer distances killed or wounded about 400 warriors during another fight.

**The Decline
of the Buffalo**

The sight of rotting buffalo was increasingly common in the Plains during the nineteenth century. White hunters who killed buffalo for sport left millions of them dead. Of the estimated 60 million buffalo that roamed the West in 1800, that number had decreased to 13 million in 1870 and to 1,000 by 1900. This forced many American Indians to accept U.S. government offers to move to reservations in return for food and supplies.

A meeting with peace commissioners was proposed in November 1867, but Red Cloud refused to negotiate until it was agreed that whites could no longer trespass on Powder River Valley. In a show of good faith, the commissioners abandoned the forts.

Red Cloud and the Plains Indians had won the battle. But when Red Cloud finally agreed to talk peace at Fort Laramie, everything changed. Life for the American Indians would never be the same.

*Red Cloud eventually became one of the most well-known
American-Indian warriors.*

A burial scaffold stands in Oklahoma to honor Cheyenne Indians killed by the U.S. Army.

ROAD TO LITTLE BIGHORN

The notion of abandoning their traditional lifestyle was agreeable to many American Indians in the 1860s. It angered and disgusted others.

THE FORT LARAMIE TREATY

Reactions were mixed when the Fort Laramie Treaty was signed in the spring of 1868. It ceded all of what is now South Dakota, including the Black Hills, to the Sioux. No white man could trespass on Powder River country without Sioux approval. But the tribes were to remain on their reservations, straying only to hunt. They were commanded to stay away from railroad construction and military posts.

The agreement destroyed a way of life that American Indians had led for centuries. Many Indians immediately recognized that the old ways of roaming the land and hunting buffalo were over. By that time, many Indians believed they could no longer prevent the spread of white expansion and U.S. military power.

The U.S. government promised to establish an agency to provide everything the American Indians

Why Kill Buffalo?

Aside from sport, why did whites feel the need to kill so many buffalo? One reason was that they used the buffalo meat to feed railroad workers traveling to the West. They also used the hides to make inexpensive belts.

William (Buffalo Bill) Cody often killed 150 buffalo in a day. Cody was hired by the Kansas-Pacific Railroad in 1878 and killed more than 4,000 buffalo during one 17-month period.

needed to make the transition to this new way of life, including education and medical facilities. The Indians were to phase out hunting and become farmers like their white counterparts. Until they became self-sufficient, the U.S. government would supply them with food.

Several tribal leaders were incensed. Sioux chiefs such as Red Cloud, Crazy Horse, and Sitting Bull believed that hunting was part of the grand design for the Sioux people. They believed that the Great Spirit had created the sacred Black Hills for the Sioux to do just that. Sitting Bull proclaimed,

> *I am a red man. If the Great Spirit had desired me to be a white man, he would have made me so in the first place. … It is not necessary for eagles to be crows. Now we are poor, but we are free. I do not wish to be shut up in a corral. All reservation Indians I have seen are worthless. They are neither red warriors nor white farmers. They are neither wolf nor dog.*[1]

In spite of these concerns, Red Cloud signed the Fort Laramie Treaty, which created the Great Sioux Reservation even after he was informed that the tribes would receive no ammunition with which to hunt. Sitting Bull was willing to give peace a chance.

ANOTHER MASSACRE

So were the Cheyenne, who were to receive guns and ammunition from the U.S. peace commissioners. Though Chief Black Kettle had remained peaceful, other Cheyenne continued to attack white settlers. In November 1868, General Sheridan sent George Custer out with the following instructions:

> *Proceed south in the direction of the Antelope Hills, thence toward the Washita River, the supposed winter seat of the hostile tribes; to destroy their villages and ponies, to kill or hang all warriors, and bring back all women and children.*[2]

Custer and his men, however, did not take the time to separate the women and children from the men. On November 27, they slaughtered 103 Cheyenne—only 11 of which were warriors. They killed dozens of women and children, capturing only 53. Black Kettle and his wife

The Dog Soldiers

One revered group of Cheyenne was known as the Dog Soldiers. These elite warriors wore a sash that trailed on the ground and carried a sacred arrow. They were armed with rifles, bows, and arrows. A treaty in 1867 at Medicine Lodge Creek in Kansas took much of the power away from Cheyenne warriors such as the Dog Soldiers.

were among the dead, as were nearly 1,000 ponies. All that saved the massacre of every Cheyenne in the village was a band of Arapaho who arrived and killed 19 soldiers.

Custer also burned the Cheyenne meat supply. The survivors of the Washita battle were summoned to nearby Fort Cobb to see Sheridan, who wanted them to surrender in return for food. Other Indians joined the reservation. And when a Comanche tribesman named Towasi said meekly to Sheridan, "Towasi, good Indian," the general replied, "The only good Indians I ever saw were dead." Lieutenant Charles

The Story of Roman Nose

Like many other cultures in the world that believe certain things give people good luck or bad luck, the American Indians had their own superstitions. For example, Roman Nose always wore a black-and-white war bonnet in battle. He believed the bonnet protected him from harm only if he did not eat food touched by metal.

During the summer of 1868, bands of hostile Indians killed 124 people in Colorado and western Kansas. The army sent Major George A. Forsyth to sign up 50 volunteers to stop the attacks. This led to a battle at Beecher Island.

Roman Nose planned to refrain from fighting, because earlier that day, someone had removed his food from a skillet with a metal fork. According to his superstition, he knew he would die. Shamed by a fellow tribesman, he put on his war bonnet and went into battle—only to be shot in the spine. He died later that night.

Had the war bonnet kept him safe during previous conflicts? And did it fail him that day because metal had touched his food? Nobody will ever know for sure.

Nordstrom later remembered the words as, "The only good Indian is a dead Indian."[3]

Is Peace Possible?

Red Cloud and fellow Sioux Chief Spotted Tail soon visited the center of American policy. They accepted an invitation to Washington, D.C., by the U.S. Indian Bureau Commissioner Ely Parker to discuss peace in April 1870. They toured the capital and met President Ulysses S. Grant.

Little was accomplished. And the differences continued to grow between chiefs such as Red Cloud who were willing to give concessions to the government and those who were not, such as Sitting Bull and Crazy Horse.

Regardless of their stance on negotiating with the government, it looked like neither side would survive long. American Indians who agreed to stay on reservations were

Red Cloud

Red Cloud may have been the most well-known American Indian in the country when he arrived in Washington, D.C., in 1870. A *New York Times* article on June 1, 1870, said that Red Cloud was "undoubtedly the most celebrated warrior now living on the American Continent. ... The friendship of Red Cloud is of more importance to the whites than that of any 10 chiefs on the plains."[4]

The Road to Statehood

Several territories were granted statehood during the U.S. government and Indian conflicts of the 1860s and 1870s. This included statehood for Kansas (1861), Nebraska (1864), Nevada (1867), and Colorado (1876). American-Indian holdouts in North Dakota and South Dakota helped prevent these territories from becoming states until 1889. Both were granted statehood on the same day.

not receiving all their provisions and were beginning to starve. Those who wished to stay free were also hungry because the buffalo that sustained them were being killed off.

Meanwhile, railroads and roads were being constructed on lands ceded to the tribes, violating the Laramie Treaty. The U.S. government simply was not keeping its promises.

Many American Indians understood their choices. They could die on reservations set up by the U.S. government, or they could fight the U.S. Army while living the way they thought the Great Spirit meant them to live. The number of American Indians who chose the latter was growing. A showdown with government soldiers was inevitable. ⌐

White men on a westbound train shoot at buffalo for sport.

Deadwood, South Dakota, emerged as a result of the Black Hills gold rush.

A People Pushed to the Edge

White expansion became unstoppable by the early 1870s. More railroads were constructed; new forts were built. Gold mining attracted prospectors. Settlers were streaming in. Millions of buffalo were being killed, and the treaties

that had given sole use of the territory
in the Plains to the Indians were being
ignored.

The Northern Pacific Railroad
had yet to reach the Northern
Plains, and the battlegrounds were
quiet. Occasional attacks by hostile
tribesmen proved to be no more than
an inconvenience.

THE SEEDS OF A SHOWDOWN

In 1873, Sioux leader Crazy Horse
encountered a force commanded
by George Custer for the first time.
A group of Sioux and Cheyenne
came upon the troops as they were
napping. The tribes attempted in
vain to run off the cavalry's herd of
horses. The Cheyenne attacked, but
it resulted in minimal loss of life.

The seeds of a showdown in the
Plains were planted in the summer of
1874. Custer and his Seventh Cavalry
were sent into the Black Hills to find
an ideal spot for a fort and a pathway

Custer in the Black Hills

George Armstrong Custer
led an expedition through
the Black Hills to find
an area appropriate for a
fort. Members included
Custer's brother Tom,
President Grant's son, and
the grandson of Samuel
Morse, the inventor of the
telegraph. The group also
brought along a 16-piece
musical band to entertain
them as they marched.

from Fort Abraham Lincoln to Fort Laramie. That road would cut through the heart of the Great Sioux Reservation, violating the Treaty of 1868. But the violation of agreements had become the rule rather than the exception.

Enough gold was discovered in the Black Hills to attract a stampede of miners. Though the government made an attempt to prevent the prospectors from infiltrating Sioux country, the Sioux were overwhelmed by white settlers seeking gold.

Lawmakers in Washington, D.C., ordered the tribes who lived in gold country to move—another violation of the Treaty of 1868. The U.S. government had now become an ally of the gold miners rather than a protector of the tribes. Within a year, more than 10,000 miners had streamed into the Black Hills.

In September 1875, a half-breed Sioux named Louis Richards arrived at Sitting Bull's camp with a letter from the U.S. government. It announced that a new peace commissioner from Washington, D.C., would be arriving at Fort Laramie with an offer to buy the Black Hills from the American Indians. The group would soon inquire about a selling price.

Sitting Bull was quick to answer. "I want you to go and tell the Great White Father that I do not wish to sell any land to the government," he said to Richards. Sitting Bull picked up a pinch of dirt and added with a forceful voice. "Not even so much as this."[1]

The Plains Indians had been lied to often enough. They were ready to make a stand. More tribesmen were becoming ready to fight for their

Strong in Peace

In 1836, a nine-year-old white girl named Cynthia Ann Parker was taken captive by Comanche warriors in Texas. Nine years later, Parker married Chief Peta Nocona of the Nocona tribe. Soon thereafter she gave birth to son Quanah.

Parker was eventually recaptured and returned to white society. Her son, Quanah, joined a warlike Comanche tribe called the Quahadi and eventually became a war chief. The Quahadi hated whites and refused to live on a reservation, opting instead to roam and hunt.

Quanah survived several battles. In the late spring of 1875, Quanah and a band of Quahadi eventually surrendered at Fort Sill when they were told they would not be imprisoned.

As fierce as Quanah was in war, he was equally strong in peace. He visited his white relatives and learned some English. He became a rancher and eventually a judge. In 1902, the man now known as Quanah Parker was elected deputy sheriff of Lawton, Oklahoma. He also created a local school district, of which he was elected president.

Through it all, he maintained his Comanche beliefs. Upon his death in 1911, a medicine man flapped his hands over Quanah's body like an eagle to send the chief's spirit into the afterlife. This was a spiritual tradition of the Comanche.

General Sheridan gained fame in battle in the American Civil War before fighting in the Indian wars.

precious territory. Meanwhile, the U.S. government was preparing to take the Black Hills by force.

During one meeting, Sioux Chief Spotted Tail asked peace commissioners what they were offering for the Black Hills. The answer was $400,000 a year or $6 million paid in 15 installments, much less than the land was worth. Spotted Tail rejected the offer.

PREPARING FOR BATTLE

Commissioner of Indian Affairs Edward P. Smith issued a demand that all Indians living freely in the Great Sioux Reservation must report to government agencies set up in that territory by January 31, 1876. Those who refused would be met by troops. This was another order that violated the Treaty of 1868.

Lieutenant General Sheridan was in charge of the army on the north and south Plains. On February 8, 1876, he ordered General George Crook and General Alfred Terry to prepare military operations around the Powder, Tongue, Rosebud, and Bighorn rivers.

The army had changed a lot since the Civil War a decade earlier. The number of soldiers had been drastically slashed and pay was poor. Diseases such as alcoholism and scurvy wiped out many men. But the Seventh Cavalry that was sent to

A Tragic Misunderstanding

In the 1800s, Plains Indians did not have calendars like the white people. So when they were informed that the government set a January 31, 1876, timetable for them to return to their reservations, they replied to their agent representative that they were hunting buffalo and that they would return by spring. By the time that answer was returned to the government, military plans against them had already begun.

Low Dog's Opinion

Oglala Sioux warrior Low Dog expressed the view of many American Indians in the 1860s and 1870s. "I heard some people talking that the chief of the white men wanted the Indians to live where he ordered and do as he said, and he would feed and clothe them. … Why should I allow any man to support me against my will anywhere, as long as I have hands and so long as I am an able man, not a boy?"[2]

battle the Plains Indians consisted of veteran soldiers. It was an elite fighting group.

So were the Sioux. Those who remained were warriors with a mission. They had lived on reservations and been stung by broken treaties. Many of them had witnessed devastating attacks on innocent villages. They were experienced and angry warriors.

General George Armstrong Custer

Actors reenact the Battle of the Little Bighorn.

A GOOD DAY
TO DIE

The brutally cold winter of 1875 and 1876 had finally given way to spring. The troops dispatched by Sheridan were tracking down Indians considered hostile. And there were certainly many different bands of Indians to track.

When the Sioux and Cheyenne defeated George Crook's regiment at the Battle of Rosebud Creek, Plains Indians from all over joined in to celebrate the victory. For nearly a week, they streamed in from reservations and other areas of the Plains to dance, feast, and swap stories about the victory. By the fourth week of June, the village had grown from 450 lodges housing 3,000 tribesmen and 800 warriors to an estimated 1,000 lodges housing 9,000 tribesmen and 3,000 warriors.

But the Battle of Rosebud Creek was not the great victory foretold in Sitting Bull's vision of hundreds of Bluecoats and Indian scouts falling from the sky into his camp as a gift from the Great Spirit. Rosebud Creek was far east of Sitting Bull's camp. An even greater victory was coming. The chiefs met and decided to move their tribes beyond the Bighorn River, where antelope herds roamed freely.

Noble Death

The relatively small number of warriors killed at the Battle of the Little Bighorn had entered the fight intending to die. A number of Sioux and Cheyenne knew that a momentous fight was inevitable and had vowed before it even began to give their lives to the cause of freedom for the American Indians.

The Arikara were traditional enemies of the Sioux and Cheyenne. They believed linking with the U.S. Army was the only way to ensure survival. Little Brave, Bloody Knife, and Bobtailed Bull were killed at the Battle of the Little Bighorn fighting alongside Major Reno.

What was left of Crook's regiment retreated, and the army groups led by Terry and Colonel John Gibbon continued stalking Sioux and Cheyenne. Scouts of a Seventh Cavalry group led by Major Marcus A. Reno spotted an Indian trail leading to Little Bighorn. General Terry ordered Gibbon's men into the field and Custer's Seventh Cavalry to pick up the trail and follow it. Terry's plan was to surround the Indians.

Custer, however, was motivated by personal glory. He marched his men 30 miles (48 km) a day in an attempt to beat Gibbon. He believed he and his Seventh Cavalry could defeat the Sioux and Cheyenne warriors by themselves. At dawn on June 25, 1876, Custer's troops noticed a pony herd that spread for miles. Seconds later, they saw the largest village of Plains Indians ever assembled.

Sioux warrior Gall survived the battle at Little Bighorn, but his wife and
three children were killed.

Custer's Plan

The troops were overwhelmed at the sight of the large Indian encampment. They warned Custer to wait for reinforcements. But Custer would have none of it. "The largest Indian camp on the North American continent is ahead and I'm going to attack it," he announced.[2]

Custer divided up his regiment. He sent Captain Frederick Benteen to scout the southern hills. He directed Reno to cross the Little Bighorn and attack

Not for Men Only

Not everyone who fought at the Battle of the Little Bighorn was male. Several women fought as well, but only a few stories of them survive in written form.

A tribeswoman named Calf Trail Woman decided she wanted to fight. A Cheyenne named Antelope Woman told the story,

A few women besides me were watching the battle. We were not there to do any fighting, but we were just looking and cheering our men with our songs. All of us had knives, and some of us had hatchets. But these were carried in our belts all the time for use in our work, not for hurting people.

Most of the women who watched the battle stayed out of the reach of the bullets, as I did. But there was one who stayed close at all times: she was Calf Trail Woman. She had a pistol with bullets, and she fired many shots at the soldiers.[1]

Antelope Woman was particularly concerned about her nephew Noisy Walking, whom she later found. He had three bullets in him—one had gone through his body—and he had been stabbed several times. He was carried back to the camp, where his father White Bull, a medicine man, tried to save him. It was too late.

from the south. Custer would run his men parallel to support Reno.

THE BATTLE BEGINS

Reno's group began to charge in, but he halted when he could not find Custer, who had ridden north without informing him. Custer's men soon met 1,500 Sioux warriors ready for battle. Custer's men retreated to find higher ground, but Crazy Horse and approximately 1,000 more Oglala and Cheyenne warriors appeared on the ridge behind the Seventh Cavalry.

Oglala warrior Low Dog sounded the battle cry, yelling, "It is a good day to die! Follow me!"[3]

Meanwhile, Reno's men attacked the Sioux camp, immediately killing Gall's wife and three children. Years later, Gall said, "It made my heart bad. After that I killed all my enemies with the hatchet."[4]

The warriors, led by Crazy Horse and Gall, wiped out many of Reno's

The Battle of the Greasy Grass

To most Americans, the showdown between Indian tribes and the Seventh Cavalry was known as the Battle of the Little Bighorn. To the Indians, it was called the Battle of the Greasy Grass—named for the area along the banks of the Little Bighorn River that was a favorite summer spot for the tribes.

men using bows and arrows and tomahawks. Reno, an inexperienced Indian fighter, ordered his men to dismount and fight, but that proved disastrous. By the time they re-mounted and retreated across the river into the bluffs, half the troops were dead.

Reno's retreat allowed Crazy Horse to send hundreds of men to join the warriors fighting Custer. As Cheyenne Chief Two Moon explained,

> We circled all around [Custer]—swirling like water round a stone. We shoot, we ride fast, we shoot again. Soldiers drop, and horses fall on them. … Indians keep swirling round and round, and the soldiers killed only a few. Many soldiers fell. … Once in a while some man would break out and run towards the river, but he would fall.

> At last about 100 men and five horse men stood on the hill all bunched together. All along the bugler kept blowing his commands. … Then a chief was killed. I hear it was [Custer], I don't know. … One man all alone ran far down toward the river, then round up over the hill. I thought he was going to escape, but a Sioux fired and hit him in the head. He was the last man.[5]

Custer was among the dead. A warrior named Bad Soup pointed him out on the ground and said, "[Custer] thought he was the greatest man in the world. Now he lies here." Fellow warrior and Sitting Bull's nephew, White Bull, answered, "If that is [Custer], I am the man who killed him."[6]

Meanwhile, Reno's regiment was struggling to stay alive. Fortunately, Benteen arrived to help organize a defensive stand. Fighting lasted into the night with more soldiers falling.

The following morning, hundreds of warriors armed with guns taken from the dead soldiers returned to attack Reno and his men. They killed more troops before Sitting Bull put a stop to it. "Let them live," he declared. "They have come against us, and we have killed a few. If we kill them all, they will send a bigger army against us."[7]

The warrior Indians had killed 260 soldiers, including 212 of Custer's men. Approximately 30 Indian warriors had lost their lives, though many more were injured.

After the Battle

The cruelty of battle did not end when the fighting stopped. Two Cheyenne women who stumbled upon Custer's dead body pushed a bone sewing awl through his ears. The symbolic gesture was done because Custer had not listened to the American Indians when they had told him years earlier he would be sorry if another treaty was broken.

The thought of revenge stayed with the Sioux and Cheyenne for quite a while. They did not celebrate their victory. Rather, they wondered what would happen next. They had won the battle, but they were afraid they were losing the war. White America was simply too powerful.

Their fears were justified. They were indeed about to lose the war, but not before white soldiers exacted revenge against them for the Battle of the Little Bighorn.

Not all the Indians at Little Bighorn fought against Custer. These Crow Indians were scouts for Custer.

A grave honors one of the dead at Little Bighorn.

WHITE FURY,
RED DEATH

day had passed after the Battle of the Little Bighorn. The stench of dead bodies and horses hung over the battlefield.

From miles away, the soldiers led by Generals Terry and Gibbon noticed figures lying on the ground. They believed they were buffalo carcasses rotting after a hunt. But as they got closer, they realized to their horror that they were dead soldiers and horses—hundreds of them.

THE NATION REACTS

Messengers took the news to forts around the area. Telegraphs sent the word throughout the country. On July 6, 1876, two days after the nation's centennial celebration, news of the battle was reported by the newspapers. White people reacted with anger and a thirst for revenge because they did not understand the motivations of the Indians and because they were fueled by the white media. They wondered, how could these "bloodthirsty savages" do such a thing?

The triumph at the Little Bighorn did not bring joy to the Indians. They could fight. They could win

Assigning Blame

Marcus Reno received most of the blame for the disaster at Little Bighorn. Some believed he should not have stopped the attack when he failed to see Custer's men. An inquiry was held in the winter of 1879 that cleared Reno, but the court of public opinion still held him mostly responsible for the disaster that struck the Seventh Cavalry.

battles. But they could not stop the U.S. government or the millions of white Americans.

Even such hardened and proud Sioux as Sitting Bull and Crazy Horse began to understand what Red Cloud had seen years earlier. They could run and they could fight, but they could not hide, especially now that the killing of Custer and the Seventh Cavalry had raised an intense anger in white people everywhere.

Custer's Wife

The strongest defender of the actions of General Custer at the Battle of the Little Bighorn was his widow, Libbie, who turned to writing after his death. Libbie continued to defend her husband until she passed away in 1933, nearly 57 years after General Custer was killed.

WHITE AMERICA STRIKES BACK

The Bluecoats were everywhere. In September, 1876, General Crook and his men attacked the Oglala village of Chief American Horse in the northern Black Hills. When Sitting Bull and Crazy Horse arrived, they saw a huge army of Bluecoats. Most of the Sioux escaped, but the soldiers then raced into the Black Hills after setting fire to the camp.

The Sioux warriors followed, but it was too late. When they arrived at their camp, it too was in flames, and many men, women, and children had been killed. "What is it the white people want?" Sitting Bull asked in despair and anger. "We have been running up and down this country, but they follow us from one place to another."[1]

The destruction of the camps was not the only disheartening news for Sitting Bull. In October, he learned that the U.S. government had forced the chiefs on the reservations to sign a treaty giving up the Black Hills and the entire Powder River Valley. Those who wished to pursue the lifestyle many

Flight of the Cheyenne

The heroic battles of 1876 turned into surrender in 1877 for the Cheyenne. The Northern Cheyenne had been told they would live in a reservation along with the Sioux, but they learned that the Indian Bureau had assigned them to move south to live with Southern Cheyenne. They had to live away from their sacred Black Hills.

In the Southern Plains, they did not receive enough food, and diseases ran rampant. Eventually, they received permission to hunt buffalo but quickly discovered that few were left.

Chief Dull Knife and his Cheyenne decided to escape to the North. They were chased by approximately 10,000 soldiers as winter began to come. Dull Knife brought his tribe to Red Cloud. But Red Cloud had long given up the fight:

Our hearts are sore for you. Many of our blood are among your dead. This has made our hearts bad. But what can we do? The Great Father is all-powerful. ... So listen to your old friend and do without complaint what the Great Father tells you.[2]

The Cheyenne fought bravely, but they were overwhelmed. Those not killed were herded back to Fort Robinson. They were eventually allowed to live on a reservation on Tongue River, but they had lost their spirit.

believed the Great Spirit had intended them to live had no choice but to accept life on the reservation or flee.

The Nez Percés

Following Little Bighorn, tribes everywhere were ordered to reservations, even those who had never hindered white expansion. Among them were the Nez Percés of the Northwest, who were led by Chief Joseph. His tribesmen had never killed a white man. They had lived in peace, but were ordered to abandon their homeland for a dismal Idaho reservation in 1877. The Nez Percés fought bravely for their freedom and killed many U.S. troops in battle despite being greatly outnumbered before they were forced to surrender.

Sitting Bull and Crazy Horse

Sitting Bull chose the latter. He and his people moved to Canada. Life there was hard. Buffalo no longer roamed in great numbers that far north. Sitting Bull's people may have lived in hunger in Canada, but they also lived in peace.

Gall returned to America in 1880, and Sitting Bull returned the following year. The government promised Sitting Bull that he could live on a reservation with his people in North Dakota, but he was arrested for the murder of Custer and placed in a stockade. Released in 1883, he eventually toured the country with Buffalo Bill Cody in the Wild West show.

Sitting Bull could not accept living in the white man's world. He eventually returned to the reservation. In 1888, when the U.S. government decided to break up the Great Sioux Reservation and give 9 million more acres (3.6 million ha) to white settlers, Sitting Bull fought against it. But his fellow tribesmen, including Gall, signed the agreement. Sitting Bull was old and alone in his anger and desire to fight for Sioux freedom.

A reporter asked Sitting Bull how the Indians felt about giving away that much land. "Indians!" he shrieked. "There are no more Indians but me."[3]

In 1877, a year after the Battle of the Little Bighorn, Crazy Horse surrendered at Camp Robinson. He eventually was arrested on a phony charge that he planned to make trouble. He angrily resisted imprisonment while wielding a knife,

The Utes

The last Plains Indian tribe to be subdued was the Utes of Colorado. Governor Frederick W. Pitkin of Colorado had used a "Utes Must Go" slogan in his campaign. Government agent Nathan Meeker attempted to turn the Utes from hunters into farmers, but the tribe resisted. A battle ensued in which 11 cavalrymen were killed. The government then forcibly removed the Utes from Colorado to a barren tract of land in Utah.

then was bayoneted to death by Private William Gentiles. Crazy Horse was 35 years old when he died.

By the 1880s, the Battle of the Little Bighorn had become legendary, and so had warriors such as Sitting Bull and Crazy Horse. Many people in white America had revered them. Whites were no longer filled with anger, mostly because they understood that the American Indians had been subdued.

Now it was simply a matter of completing the job. The Indian wars would soon be over. A slaughter in South Dakota finally ended the struggle. ⌐

*An American Indian touches the feather of a golden eagle to a
monument honoring those who died in the battle.*

A Ghost Dance shirt was supposed to protect its wearer from harm.

A New Hope?

t was October 1890. Sitting Bull sat in
the log cabin he had built in the Standing
Rock Reservation on which he and his tribe had been
forced to live. He was a beaten man. Hunger, disease,
and death were all around him.

THE GHOST DANCE

One day, a tribesman named Kicking Bear entered the cabin. He told Sitting Bull about a Paiute Indian named Wovoka who had been sent back to Earth by the Great Spirit. Wovoka had returned to teach American Indians a magic dance called the Ghost Dance. It would allow Indians to see their dead relatives and restore the old ways of life.

Not only that, but the Ghost Dance would bring all the buffalo to life as well and bury the white man beneath a great rain. The Indians would again be free to roam the land and hunt in great numbers. They would live in happiness.

Kicking Bear claimed he had danced the Ghost Dance in the middle of an empty plain. He had then seen and spoken to many dead friends, and a herd of buffalo appeared. He said he had killed one with a bow and arrow

Gall's Death

Sioux Chief Gall did not meet a violent end, as did Sitting Bull and Crazy Horse. Gall became a leader of his reservation before dying peacefully in 1893. Though vehemently opposed to reservation life, he eventually accepted it and served as a justice of the Indian Police Court on Standing Rock Reservation before passing away at age 53.

and had shared it in a buffalo feast. He added that the buffalo bones then formed again into a new living buffalo.

The excited Kicking Bear claimed that he could teach Sitting Bull the Ghost Dance. Sitting Bull, however, was quite skeptical. He did not believe the dead could return to life. But his fellow tribesmen convinced Sitting Bull to allow Kicking Bear to teach them the dance.

Soon the Ghost Dance was being performed throughout the reservation. Even

Words from the Other Side

The treatment of the American Indians was eventually deemed unfair by many of those who had shared responsibility for it. Among them was General Crook, who said that the various tribes had been wronged throughout the Indian War.

Crook had stalked the Sioux and Cheyenne before losing a brief conflict days before the Battle of the Little Bighorn. Three years later, he expressed sadness at the way the American Indians had been treated:

Greed and avarice on the part of the Whites, in other words the Almighty Dollar, is at the bottom of nine tenths of all our Indian troubles.[1]

U.S. Army Colonel Richard Dodge issued a similar comment:

Next to the crime of slavery the foulest blot on [the reputation] of the Government of the Unites States is its treatment of the [American Indians].[2]

Even General Philip Sheridan eventually changed his attitude:

We took away their country and their means of support, broke up their mode of living, their habits of life, introduced disease and decay among them, and it was for this and against this that they made war. Could anyone expect less?[3]

Red Cloud, who had given up any
hope of a return to the chosen
American-Indian lifestyle, had
become a believer.

Wovoka instructed the Ghost
Dancers to wear special shirts painted
white with drawings of buffalo, eagles,
stars, and moons. Those wearing
the shirts could not be harmed. The
Ghost Dancers were instructed not to
fight the white man, even if the tribes
were attacked. They were simply to
perform the Ghost Dance until they
were saved.

THE MASSACRE AT WOUNDED KNEE

Some reservation agents
understood that the dance was an act
of desperation by the Indians. Others
were frightened by this strange new
dance, including Pine Ridge agent
D.F. Royer. A nervous man, the
Indians had named Royer the Young-
Man-Afraid-of-the-Sioux. Royer sent
a telegraph to government officials in

Jumping Bull

Among the Sioux who
surrounded the cabin to
protect Sitting Bull before
he was arrested was his
nephew, Jumping Bull. He
was the same tribesman
who had cut 100 pieces
of flesh off Sitting Bull
during the Sun Dance
celebration right before
the Battle of the Little
Bighorn. That sacrificial
ritual allowed Sitting Bull
to see a vision that a great
Sioux victory over the
Bluecoats was about to
take place.

Washington, D.C., stating:

Indians are dancing in the snow and are wild and crazy. We need protection and we need it now. We need at least a thousand soldiers, maybe more.[4]

The American Indian Movement

The massacre at Wounded Knee returned to the spotlight on February 27, 1973. On that day, the American Indian Movement (AIM), a group of young militant Indians, symbolically seized the town of Wounded Knee, South Dakota, to protest the mistreatment of American Indians. The U.S. Marshals Service eventually took control of the town on May 8, but not before two AIM members were dead. One marshal and one FBI agent were wounded in the struggle.

Troops were dispatched to Pine Ridge. The government was particularly fearful of Sitting Bull. Agent James McLaughlin decided to send Sioux policemen who had sided with the government to arrest Sitting Bull. Sioux tribesmen with whom Sitting Bull had grown up began to take him away.

But outside the cabin, he saw that approximately 100 fellow Sioux had gathered to fight for him. Sitting Bull then resisted arrest. A deaf warrior named Black Coyote shot and killed an Indian policeman named Bull Head. Aiming at another policeman, Black Coyote missed and hit Sitting Bull. The great chief died at the age of 56.

Sitting Bull's fight for the Sioux nation had ended. And in South Dakota, a massacre would end the Indian War.

That horrible story began when the fearful U.S. government banned the Ghost Dance. The Seventh Cavalry, which included the few survivors of Little Bighorn more than a decade earlier, was dispatched to stop the dancing, which they believed was a prelude to an uprising. Colonel James Forsyth was told to peacefully bring in the Ghost Dancers. They would then be taken to a military prison in Omaha, Nebraska.

Forsyth and his men surrounded the village on December 29, 1890, at Wounded Knee Creek. His men arrived that day and ordered the Sioux to turn in their weapons. The Sioux began the Ghost Dance in the belief that it would protect them from harm.

After the Massacre

Following the slaughter of an estimated 300 American Indians at Wounded Knee, many of the dead bodies of men, women, and children were carried into a nearby church. Ironically, a sign was hanging above the pulpit. It read, "PEACE ON EARTH, GOOD WILL TO MEN."[5]

Black Coyote shot his rifle into the air and was pushed by a soldier. The gun went off again. When the smoke cleared, a soldier lay dead. Bullets began to fly. Most of the Sioux were unarmed. The result was a massacre. An estimated 300 men, women, and children were killed immediately or left to die.

And just as those American Indians were buried in the snow, so were the hopes and dreams of their people. Perhaps Red Cloud stated it best:

> *They made us many promises, more than I can remember. But they never kept but one; they promised to take our land, and they took it.*[6] ⌐

Commemorations of the massacre at Wounded Knee are still held near
this sign, which tells what happened on that fateful day.

TIMELINE

1492	1842	1848
Christopher Columbus and fellow explorers land in the Americas.	The great white migration to the West begins on the Oregon Trail.	The California Gold Rush begins, bringing more white trespassers through American-Indian land.

1862	1862	1864
The Homestead Act provides cheap land for white settlers.	Santee Sioux in Minnesota go on a rampage in August, killing an estimated 500 white settlers.	Men led by Colonel John Chivington massacre Cheyenne and Arapaho villagers in Colorado on November 29.

1851	1854	1857
The Treaty of 1851 establishes American Indians' dependence on the U.S. government for food and supplies.	On August 19, John Grattan's men open fire on a village and are killed by Sioux warriors.	Approximately 10,000 Lakota Sioux gather and hold the first Indian grand council.

1866	1867	1868
An estimated 2,000 Sioux wipe out a group of soldiers in Wyoming on December 21.	The U.S. government sends a peace commission to meet with Sioux tribes in Nebraska.	The Fort Laramie Treaty of 1868 cedes all of the Black Hills to the Sioux.

TIMELINE

1868	1870	1874
On November 27, General Custer and his men kill 103 Cheyenne in the Battle of Washita.	Red Cloud and a group of Sioux go to Washington, D.C., to discuss peace.	General Custer and his Seventh Cavalry discover gold in the Black Hills.

1876	1876	1876
Sitting Bull and his Sioux participate in the Sun Dance ritual in early June.	On June 17, the tribes attack Crook and his men at Rosebud Creek.	General Custer and an estimated 300 cavalrymen are killed in the Battle of the Little Bighorn on June 25.

1875

The U.S. government demands that all American Indians in the Black Hills move to reservations.

1876

The deadline passes for the Sioux to report to reservations. The U.S. government declares war on all "hostile" Indians.

1876

General George Crook and his men attack a Cheyenne village on March 17.

1877

Congress takes the Black Hills away from the American Indians and forces them onto the Great Sioux Reservation.

1889

The Ghost Dance spreads throughout American-Indian reservations, promising to resurrect the Indian nation.

1890

Soldiers massacre about 300 Lakota men, women, and children at Wounded Knee Creek on December 29.

ESSENTIAL FACTS

DATE OF EVENT

June 25, 1876

PLACE OF EVENT

Little Bighorn River at Crow Agency, Montana

KEY PLAYERS

❖ General George Custer, Seventh Cavalry
❖ Major Marcus Reno, Seventh Cavalry
❖ Sitting Bull, Sioux chief
❖ Crazy Horse, Sioux chief

Highlights of Event

❖ White settlers began migrating west in the early 1840s.

❖ The discovery of gold in California added to numbers of white travelers passing through American-Indian territory.

❖ Thousands of American Indians and U.S. soldiers were killed during various conflicts, adding to tensions.

❖ American-Indian mistrust was fueled by violations of the Treaties of 1851 and 1868.

❖ The discovery of gold in the Black Hills brought white travelers into the heart of Sioux and Cheyenne country. Gold seekers and other whites were attacked daily.

❖ American Indians refused to sell the U.S. Government the Black Hills. Officials in Washington, D.C., declared war on "hostile" Indians.

Quote

"[Custer] thought he was the greatest man in the world. Now he lies here."—*Bad Soup, Sioux warrior who fought in the Battle of the Little Bighorn*

ADDITIONAL RESOURCES

SELECT BIBLIOGRAPHY

Brown, Dee. *Bury My Heart at Wounded Knee*. New York: Henry Holt and Company, 1970.

Lewis, Jon E. *The Mammoth Book of Native Americans*. New York: Carroll & Graf Publishers, 2004.

McMurtry, Larry. *Crazy Horse*. New York: Lipper/Viking, 1999.

Sajna, Mike. *Crazy Horse: The Life Behind the Legend*. Edison, NJ: Castle Books, 2005.

Taylor, William O. *With Custer on the Little Bighorn*. New York: Penguin Books, 1996.

Viola, Herman J. *It is a Good Day to Die: Indian Eyewitnesses Tell the Story of the Battle of the Little Bighorn*. New York: Crown Publishers, Inc., 1998.

Viola, Herman J. *Little Bighorn Remembered*. New York: Times Books, 1999.

Warren Ferrell, Nancy. *The Battle of the Little Bighorn in American History*. Springfield, NJ: Enslow Publishers, Inc., 1996.

FURTHER READING

Ferrell, Nancy Warren. *The Battle of the Little Bighorn in American History*. Springfield, NJ: Enslow Publishers, Inc., 1996.

Goble, Paul. *Red Hawk's Account of Custer's Last Battle: The Battle of Little Bighorn*. Lincoln, NE: University of Nebraska Press, 1992.

Knowlton, Marylee, and Michael V. Uschaw. *The Battle of the Little Bighorn: Events That Shaped America*. Milwaukee, WI: Gareth Stevens Publishing, 2002.

Nichols, Ron H. *Men With Custer: Biographies of the 7th Cavalry*. Hardin, MT: Custer Battlefield Historical Museum Association, 2000.

Reef, Catherine. *Buffalo Soldiers*. New York: Twenty-First Century Books, 1993.

WEB SITES

To learn more about The Battle of the Little Bighorn, visit
ABDO Publishing Company on the World Wide Web at
www.abdopublishing.com. Web sites about The Battle of the
Little Bighorn are featured on our Book Links page. These links
are routinely monitored and updated to provide the most current
information available.

PLACES TO VISIT

Crazy Horse Memorial
U.S. Highway 16/385, SD 57730
605-673-4681
www.crazyhorse.org
See the ongoing sculpting of Crazy Horse into a Black Hills
mountain and visit the Indian Museum of North America,
featuring displays of Native American culture both yesterday and
today.

Custer Battlefield Museum
Garryowen, MT 59031
406-638-2000
www.custermuseum.org
Featuring re-enactment of the Battle of the Little Bighorn, as well
as Little Bighorn National Monument and both Native American
and U.S. Cavalry artifacts.

Wounded Knee Museum
Exit 110, Interstate 90, Wall, SD 57790
605-279-2573
www.woundedkneemuseum.org
This narrative museum tells the story of the massacre at Wounded
Knee through exhibits and photos.

Glossary

American Indians
A term for all Indians who populated America before it was discovered by European explorers.

Black Hills
A mountainous region of the Midwest that the Sioux believed was given to them as a gift from the Great Spirit.

Bluecoats
The English translation of a Sioux term for the U.S. Cavalry.

cavalry
The U.S. army group most responsible for fighting the Indian War of the mid-to late-1800s.

Cheyenne
An American-Indian tribe that populated much of the Western Plains during the 1800s.

fort
A fortified building occupied by troops preparing for contact with the enemy.

Ghost Dance
The mystical dance performed by American Indians in 1889 and 1890 that was intended to magically bring dead tribe members back to life and drown all white people in a great flood.

Great Spirit
The entity that provided the moon, earth, sun, and sky, according to Sioux beliefs.

Lakota
A Plains Sioux division that featured seven tribes, including the Oglala and Hunkpapa.

miner
A person who traveled to seek out gold that had been discovered in various parts of the country.

Paha Sapa
> Sioux word for the Black Hills of the Dakotas.

plains
> The vast area of the Midwest settled by Cheyenne, Sioux, and other American-Indian tribes in the 1800s.

regiment
> A specific army or cavalry group responsible to carry out a mission.

scout
> An individual working for an American-Indian tribe or cavalry regiment sent out to locate the enemy prior to an anticipated battle.

Sioux
> A prominent American Indian tribe that included chiefs Sitting Bull and Crazy Horse.

Sun Dance
> A 12-day ritual performed by Sioux tribes to ask the Great Spirit for a bountiful year.

treaty
> An agreement between two conflicting sides such as the American Indians and the U.S. government that is designed to solve conflicts.

tribe
> Any American-Indian group.

Wakan Tanka
> The world's mysteries such as the earth, moon, sun, and sky, and provided by the Great Spirit, according to Sioux religious thought.

warrior
> An American Indian involved in battles.

Source Notes

Chapter 1. On the Trail to a Showdown

1. Sheila Black. *Sitting Bull and the Battle of the Little Bighorn*. Englewood, NY: Silver Burdett Press, 1989. 85.

2. Herman J. Viola. *Little Bighorn Remembered: The Untold Indian Story of Custer's Last Stand*. New York: Times Books, 1999. 134.

Chapter 2. American Indians Meet New Americans

None.

Chapter 3. Broken Treaties, Heightened Tension

1. John E. Lewis. *The Mammoth Book of Native Americans*. New York: Carroll & Graf Publishers, 2004. 147.

2. Ibid. 152.

Chapter 4. Let Them Eat Grass

1. Dee Brown. *Bury My Heart at Wounded Knee*. New York: Henry Holt and Company, 1970. 180.

2. Ibid. 38.

3. John E. Lewis. *The Mammoth Book of Native Americans*. New York: Carroll & Graf Publishers, 2004. 172.

4. Dee Brown. *Bury My Heart at Wounded Knee*. New York: Henry Holt and Company, 1970. 79.

Chapter 5. Massacre at Sand Creek

1. Herman J. Viola. *Little Bighorn Remembered: The Untold Story of Custer's Last Stand*. New York: Times Books, 1999. 5.

2. Laurie Moseley. *History and Archeology of the Red River War*, Texas Archeology Society, 9 Mar. 2007. 24 Apr. 2007 <http://www.txarch.org/arch/articles/redriver.html>.

3. Herman J. Viola. *Little Bighorn Remembered: The Untold Story of Custer's Last Stand*. New York: Times Books, 1999. 10.

4. Mike Sajna. *Crazy Horse: The Life Behind the Legend*. Edison, NJ: Castle Books, 2005. 201.

Chapter 6. Road to Little Bighorn

1. Herman J. Viola. *It is a Good Day to Die: Indian Eyewitnesses Tell the Story of the Battle of the Little Bighorn*. New York: Crown Publishers, Inc., 1998. 7.

2. Dee Brown. *Bury My Heart at Wounded Knee*. New York: Henry Holt and Company, 1970. 168.

3. Ibid. 172.

4. Mike Sajna. *Crazy Horse: The Life Behind the Legend*. Edison, NJ: Castle Books, 2005. 222.

Chapter 7. A People Pushed to the Edge

1. Sheila Black. *Sitting Bull and the Battle of the Little Bighorn*. Englewood Cliffs, NY: Silver Burdett Press, 1989. 80.

2. Herman J. Viola. *It is a Good Day to Die: Indian Eyewitnesses Tell the Story of the Battle of the Little Bighorn*. New York: Crown Publishers, Inc., 1998. 20.

Chapter 8. A Good Day to Die

1. Herman J. Viola. *It is a Good Day to Die: Indian Eyewitnesses Tell The Story of the Battle of the Little Bighorn*. New York: Crown Publishers, Inc., 1998. 73.

2. Jon E. Lewis. *The Mammoth Book of Native Americans*. New York: Carroll & Graf Publishers, 2004. 256–257.

3. Herman J. Viola. *It is a Good Day to Die: Indian Eyewitnesses Tell the Story of the Battle of the Little Bighorn*. New York: Crown Publishers, Inc., 1998. 47.

4. Dee Brown. *Bury My Heart at Wounded Knee*. New York: Henry Holt and Company, 1970. 294.

5. Jon E. Lewis. *The Mammoth Book of Native Americans*. New York: Carroll & Graf Publishers, 2004. 258–259.

6. Ibid. 261.

Source Notes Continued

7. Herman J. Viola. *It is a Good Day to Die: Indian Eyewitnesses Tell the Story of the Battle of the Little Bighorn*. New York: Crown Publishers, Inc., 1998. 73.

Chapter 9. White Fury, Red Death

1. Sheila Black. *Sitting Bull and the Battle of the Little Bighorn*. Englewood Cliffs, NJ: Silver Burdett Press, 1989. 99.

2. Dee Brown. *Bury My Heart at Wounded Knee*. New York: Henry Holt & Company, 1970. 344.

3. Sheila Black. *Sitting Bull and the Battle of the Little Bighorn*. Englewood Cliffs, NJ: Silver Burdett Press, 1989. 118.

Chapter 10. A New Hope?

1. William O. Taylor. *With Custer on the Little Bighorn*. New York: Penguin Books, 1996. 159.

2. Ibid.

3. National Park Service: Little Bighorn Battlefield National Monument, May 2000. 1 May 2007 <http://www.nps.gov/archive/libi/plains.html>.

4. Sheila Black. *Sitting Bull and the Battle of the Little Bighorn*. Englewood Cliffs, NJ: Silver Burdett Press, 1989. 123.

5. Dee Brown. *Bury My Heart at Wounded Knee*. New York: Henry Holt & Company, 1970. 445.

6. Ibid. 449.

INDEX

ABOUT THE AUTHOR

Martin Gitlin is a veteran writer based in Cleveland, Ohio. He worked as a newspaper reporter for 18 years before turning his attention to freelancing. He has won more than 45 awards, including first place for general excellence from Associated Press in 1995. That organization selected him as one of the top four feature writers in Ohio in 2001. His interests include sports, history, and classic rock music.

PHOTO CREDITS